BRAMBLE
AND THE
QUEST FOR THE HIDDEN HOARD

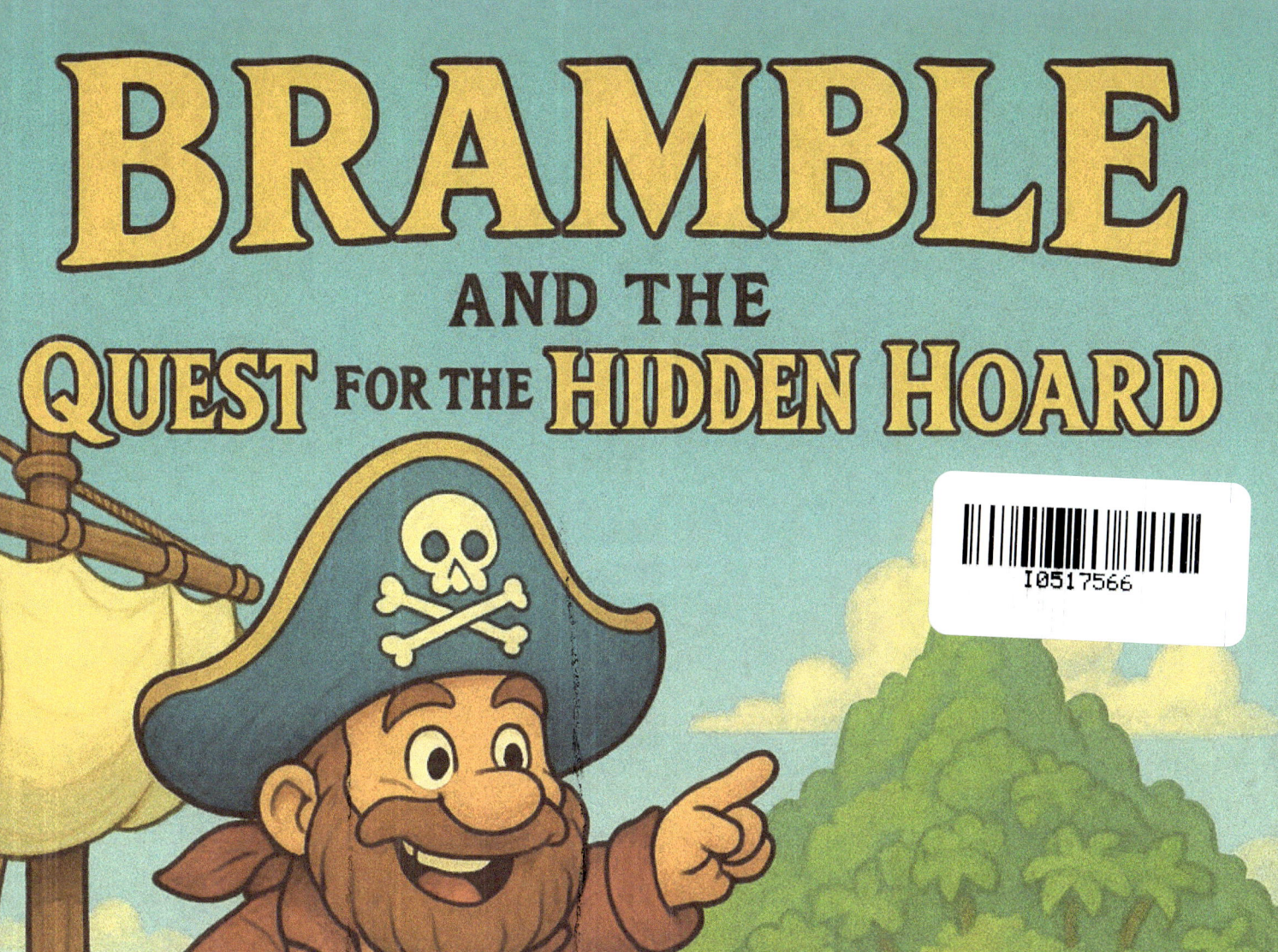

By Christine Leger

Bartholomew Bramble, or Bart as he preferred, wasn't your typical fearsome pirate. He was more of a...friendly pirate. He preferred helping old ladies cross the street to plundering, and his greatest treasure was his best friend, Sausage, the most loyal, and definitely the longest, wiener dog on the seven seas.

One breezy afternoon, while strolling through the bustling Port of Penwyth, a glint of glass caught Bart's eye. A bottle! Inside, nestled amongst the sand and seaweed, was a very old, very dusty map!

2

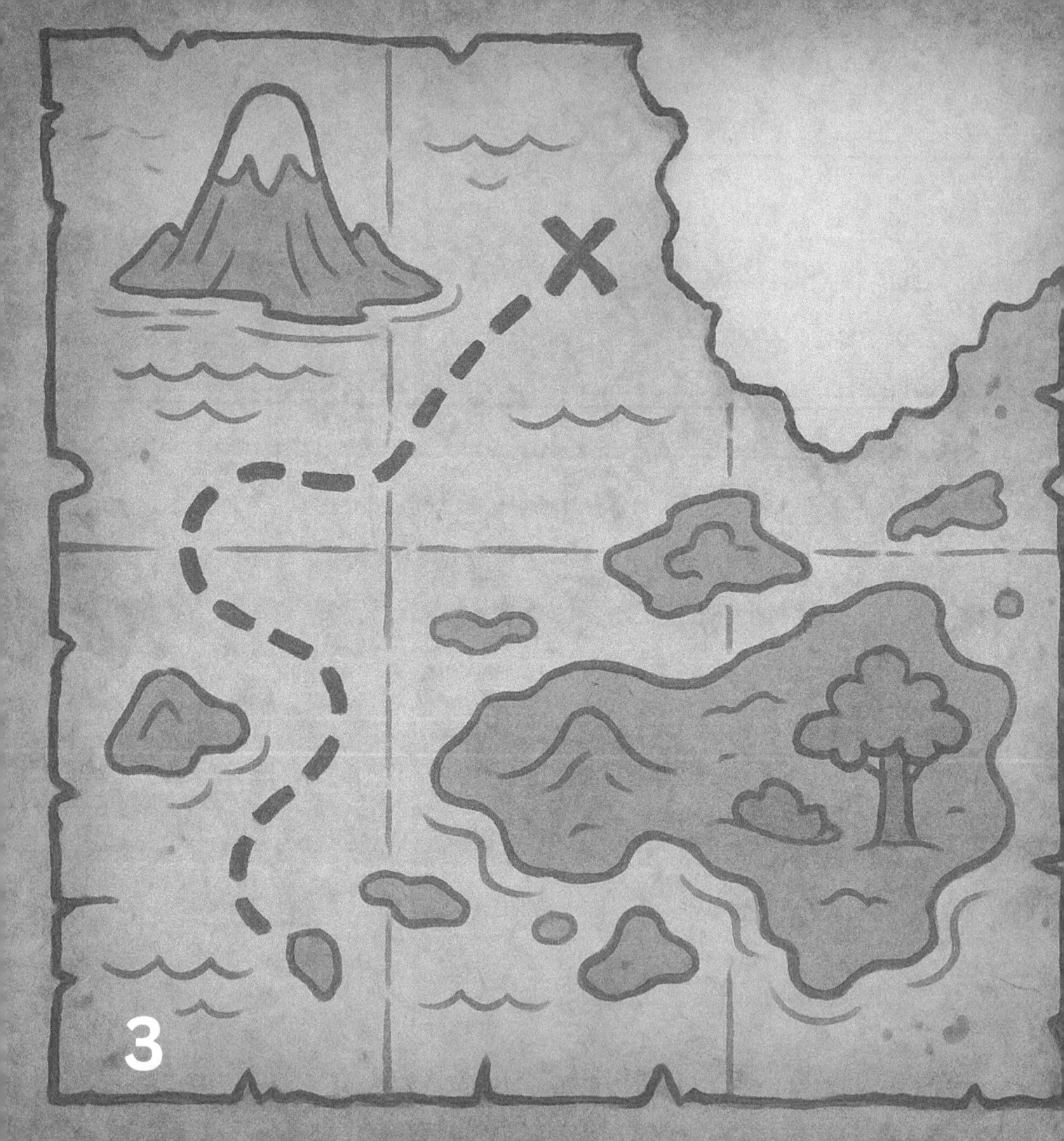

"Blimey, Sausage! A treasure map!" Bart exclaimed, unrolling the brittle parchment. Sausage barked excitedly, his tail wagging so hard his whole body wiggled. But Bart's grin faltered.

"Blast it all! A piece is missing!" The map showed a swirl of islands, treacherous straits, and a big, bold X marking what was surely the location of the hidden hoard. But without the missing piece, the X might as well have been marking a spot in his own backyard!

4

5

"Right, Sausage. Our quest begins! According to this faded writing, our first stop is...the Isle of the Talking Turtles!" Bart declared, hoisting the sails of "The Salty Sausage," his trusty, if slightly leaky, little ship.

With Sausage barking encouragement from the bow, they set sail, the wind carrying them towards a verdant island shimmering on the horizon.

6

7

The Isle of the Talking Turtles was exactly as promised – teeming with turtles! But one turtle stood apart. He was ancient, wise, and wore a pair of spectacles perched precariously on his snout.

"Greetings, young pirate," the turtle boomed, his voice like the rustling of leaves.

"I am Archibald. You seek the missing piece of the map, eh?"

9

"Indeed, Archibald! But how did you know?" Bart asked, bewildered. Archibald chuckled. "This island has seen many a treasure hunter, Bartholomew.

But knowledge isn't given freely. I shall test your wit. Answer my riddles, and the location of the missing piece shall be yours!"

Archibald posed his riddles, each more perplexing than the last. Bart racked his brain, his brow furrowed in concentration.

"What has an eye, but cannot see?" Archibald asked.

Bart pondered, tapping his chin. "A needle!" he declared triumphantly.

"Correct! Now, what is always coming, but never arrives?"

"Tomorrow!" Bart shouted, his confidence growing.

13

After several more challenging riddles, Bart had proven his cleverness.

Archibald smiled. "Well done, young pirate! The missing piece lies hidden in a small cave, nestled near the whispering palms on the western shore. But beware, the straits ahead are treacherous!"

The journey to the next clue led them through the Ghost Ships Lament, a stretch of sea shrouded in perpetual fog and haunted by the spectral remains of lost vessels. The whispering winds carried mournful tales of sailors swallowed by the sea. It was a spooky place, even for a pirate.

16

17

SEA SERPENT

Suddenly, another ship emerged from the fog – "The Sea Serpent," captained by the formidable Captain Marisol, a pirate known for her cunning and her ruthlessness.

"Ahoy there!" she called out, her voice cutting through the mist. "Looking for the hidden hoard, are we? I wouldn't mind a little company...or perhaps a little competition!"

19

Bart knew he couldn't trust Captain Marisol. He needed to outsmart her and reach the next clue first. A thrilling chase ensued, "The Salty Scamp" darting and weaving through the fog, Bart using his knowledge of the winds and currents to stay one step ahead of the larger, more powerful "Sea Serpent."

21

Finally, they escaped the clutches of Captain Marisol and arrived at Merfolk Bay, a place of shimmering beauty and enchanting melodies.

Mermaids, with their flowing hair and iridescent tails, swam around "The Salty Sausage," their songs echoing across the water.

Bart was greeted by Luna, a kind and curious mermaid who ruled the bay. "Welcome, Bartholomew Bramble," she sang, her voice like the gentle lapping of waves.

"I know why you're here. The key to the missing piece lies within the song of the conch shell. But it has been stolen by the grumpy Grotto Goblin!"

Without hesitation, Bart dove into the depths, Sausage bravely swimming alongside him in a custom-made diving helmet. They found the Grotto Goblin's lair, a dark and murky cave.

The Goblin, surprised by their arrival, reluctantly surrendered the conch shell after Bart offered him a shiny button in exchange.

Back in the bay, Luna held the conch shell to her lips and sang a magical song. The notes swirled and danced in the air, forming an image – a hidden cove on a nearby island! Bart thanked Luna profusely, promising to protect the ocean and its creatures.

29

With the final piece of the map secured, Bart pieced it together. The X was now clearly marked...in the heart of the Jungle of Jovial Jasper! But just as they were about to set sail, they heard a familiar voice...

31

"Well, well, Bartholomew Bramble," Captain Marisol sneered, her ship looming large beside "The Salty Scamp."

"Looks like I caught up with you after all. Hand over the map!"

33

Instead of fighting, Bart tried a different approach. "Captain Marisol," he said, his voice steady, "we both want the same treasure. But the map is tricky, and the jungle is dangerous. Why not work together? We can split the treasure fairly once we find it."

Captain Marisol considered his offer. After a moment, a grudging smile spread across her face. "Alright, Bramble," she said. "I'll join forces with you...for now."

34

35

And so, an unlikely alliance was formed. Bart, Sausage, Captain Marisol, and their crews entered the Jungle of Jovial Jasper, a place filled with vibrant colours, strange sounds, and mischievous creatures.

Deep within the jungle, they encountered Kiwi, a wise-cracking parrot who claimed to know the way to the treasure. "Greetings, landlubbers!" Kiwi squawked.

"I will guide you, but only if you prove yourselves worthy! You must answer my questions and overcome the jungle's challenges!"

39

Kiwi led them through a series of trials. They had to cross a treacherous rope bridge swaying high above a ravine, solve a riddle carved into ancient stones, and navigate a maze of thorny vines.

Through it all, Bart and Captain Marisol began to trust each other, realizing that teamwork was the key to survival.

Suddenly, a giant snake slithered into their path, its eyes fixed on Sausage! Everyone froze, but Sausage stood firm, barking fiercely at the reptile. Surprisingly, the snake chuckled. "I admire your courage, little dog," he said.

"You may pass. I know the jungle tests those who seek its secrets." Sausage, delighted with his bravery, wagged his tail proudly.

43

Finally, they reached the coast and discovered the Vanishing Island! This island only appeared once every decade, shrouded in mist and guarded by ancient magic. As they watched, the island slowly rose from the depths, revealing its secrets.

44

On the shore of the Vanishing Island they met Barnacle Bill, a grumpy but wise hermit crab who was the island's guardian. "You seek the treasure of Graceful Falls?" he grumbled.

"Only those who are truly worthy may claim it. And only by working together." He offered them a small golden key. "This will unlock the way."

Barnacle Bill led them to Graceful Falls, where a powerful waterfall cascaded down a cliff face. Behind the waterfall, a large boulder blocked the entrance to a hidden cave.

Using all their strength, Bart, Captain Marisol, Sausage (who helped by pushing with his nose), and Barnacle Bill worked together to move the boulder, revealing the entrance to the treasure chamber!

48

49

Inside the cave, they found it – the hidden hoard! Chests overflowed with gold coins, sparkling jewels, and ancient artifacts. It was more treasure than they could have ever imagined!

51

True to their word, Bart and Captain Marisol divided the treasure equally. They were both rich beyond their wildest dreams!

As they prepared to sail back to their respective ports, Bart and Captain Marisol realized something. They had faced dangers, solved riddles, and even made a new friend in a hermit crab. They didn't want to say goodbye.

So, they made a decision. They would combine their crews and sail the seas together, searching for new adventures, helping those in need, and always looking out for each other.

Bart, the friendly pirate, had not only found a treasure, but also a true friend. And Sausage, the loyal wiener dog, had a whole new crew to wiggle his tail at! The end.

www.ingramcontent.com/pod-product-compliance
Lightning Source LLC
Chambersburg PA
CBHW081009120626
46546CB00010B/3079